# Today Is a Cold Day

by Martha E. H. Rustad

Pebble®

CAPSTONE PRESS
a capstone imprint

Pebble Books are published by Capstone Press,
1710 Roe Crest Drive, North Mankato, Minnesota 56003
www.mycapstone.com

**Library of Congress Cataloging-in-Publication Data**
Cataloging-in-Publication data is on file with the Library of Congress.
ISBN 978-1-5157-4924-0 (library binding)
ISBN 978-1-4966-0947-2 (paperback)
ISBN 978-1-4966-0954-0 (eBook PDF)

# Note to Parents and Teachers

The What Is the Weather Today? series supports national
curriculum standards for science related to weather. This book
describes and illustrates a cold day. The images support early
readers in understanding the text. The repetition of words and
phrases helps early readers learn new words. This book also
introduces early readers to subject-specific vocabulary words,
which are defined in the Glossary section. Early readers may need
assistance to read some words and to use the Table of Contents,
Glossary, Read More, Internet Sites, and Index sections of the book.

Printed and bound in the USA.
010060S17

# Table of Contents

# How's the Weather?

Today is a cold day. The temperature is low on a cold day. Let's find out how cold it is.

TODAY

41° F

| SUN | MON | TUE | WED | THU | FRI | SAT |
|-----|-----|-----|-----|-----|-----|-----|
| 41°F | 36°F | 30°F | 38°F | 33°F | 27°F | 19°F |
| (5°C) | (2°C) | (-1°C) | (3°C) | (1°C) | (-3°C) | (-7°C) |

We can check the forecast. It tells us what the weather will be like. The numbers tell us the temperature. The numbers are smaller on cold days.

fall

winter

The forecast also shows patterns. Sometimes it is cold for more than one day. Fall and winter have a lot of cold days.

# What Do We See?

We see our breath on a cold day.

The air inside our bodies

is warm. The air outside is cold.

Our breath looks like a cloud

in the cold air.

We sometimes see rain on a cold day.

Rain turns into snow if

the temperature is cold enough.

Water freezes at 32 degrees

Fahrenheit (0 degrees Celsius).

We see frost on a
cold day. We also see ice
in puddles, rivers, and lakes.
A whole lake will freeze
if the weather stays cold.

goose bumps

# What Do We Do?

Brr! Cold air makes us shiver.
We have goose bumps. We wear
a coat to play outside
on a cold day.

Very, very cold weather

can cause frostbite.

We put on warm clothes.

A hat, scarf, and mittens

cover our skin.

At the end of a cold day,

we eat warm soup for dinner.

Let's check the forecast for tomorrow!

# Glossary

breath—the air you breathe in and out of your lungs

forecast—a prediction of what the weather will be

frost—a thin layer of ice crystals; frost forms outside in freezing weatherw

frostbite—frozen skin

goose bumps—tiny bumps that appear on people's skin when they are cold or frightened

pattern—several things that are repeated in the same way several times

shiver—to shake because of cold

temperature—the measured heat or cold of something; temperature is measured with a thermometer

# Read More

**Schuetz, Kristin.** *Forecasts.* Understanding Weather. Minneapolis: Bellwether Media, 2016.

**Schuh, Mari.** *I Feel Fall Weather.* Observing Fall. Minneapolis: Lerner Publications, 2017.

**VanVoorst, Jenny Fretland.** *Weather in Winter.* What Happens in Winter? Minneapolis: Bullfrog Books, 2017.

# Internet Sites

FactHound offers a safe, fun way to find Internet sites related to this book. All of the sites on FactHound have been researched by our staff.

Here's all you do:

Visit *www.facthound.com*

Type in this code: 9781515749240

Super-cool stuff!

Check out projects, games and lots more at **www.capstonekids.com**

# Index

**Editorial Credits**
Marissa Kirkman, editor; Charmaine Whitman and Peggie Carley, designers;
Tracey Engel, media researcher; Katy LaVigne, production specialist

**Image Credits**
Glow Images: Bele Olmez, 16 (inset); Shutterstock: Aleksey Stemmer, 14, Aleksey
Vanin, 6 (weather icons), Amy Nichole Harris, 18, Andrey Arkusha, 1, 10, iofoto, 8
(right), Juriah Mosin, 20, Kseniia Neverkovska, cover and interior design element,
Lopolo, 8 (left), MANDY GODBEHEAR, 16, Nebojsa Markovic, 12, Ozerina Anna,
cover and interior design element, Sergey Novikov, 4, Syda Productions, front cover,
vinz89, 6 (thermometer)